A YEAR OF MINI-MOVES FOR THE IN-SYNC CHILD

insyncchild.com

Every day, a move experience that lasts lifetime!

JOYE NEWMAN, M.A., and CAROL STOCK KRANOWITZ, M.A.

A Year of Mini-Moves for the In-Sync Child

All marketing and publishing rights guaranteed to and reserved by:

Sensory World
A proud imprint of Future Horizons

Toll-free: 800-489-0727 | Fax: 817-277-2270

www.SensoryWorld.com | info@sensoryworld.com

© 2021 Joye Newman and Carol Stock Kranowitz

Printed in Canada.

ISBN: 9781949177800

MOVEMENT GETS US IN SYNC!

When children play outside, climb trees, jump in puddles, and roll down hills, they develop essential sensory, perceptual, and visual skills. (See below.) Kids' daily movement diet should include all sorts of physical activities like these.

The "Mini-Moves" in this calendar are like snacks in a child's movement diet. Think of them as appetizers that introduce the main course. Every child—the sedentary one, the constant mover, and all those in-between—needs nourishing movement to feel confident and competent in his body.

Each of these Mini-Moves develops and enhances one or more of the skills defined below. Start with our tidbits and see where your imaginations take you!

FUNDAMENTAL IN-SYNC CHILD SKILLS

Sensory Skills

Tactile processing is receiving sensations through the skin and hair and responding to those sensations. A child whose brain accurately interprets tactile input is comfortable touching and being touched by other people or objects.

Vestibular processing is taking in sensations about gravity through the inner ear and responding to these sensations. The child learns where her head is relative to the surface of the earth—whether she is upright, lying down, or falling.

Proprioception is the unconscious awareness of sensations coming from muscles and joints. The child learns whether he is stomping or tiptoeing, how hard to press a pencil, and how to stretch out his arm to open a door.

Perceptual Skills

Balance, both static (being in place) and dynamic (moving), helps a child remain seated or hop across the room. Bilateral coordination is the ability to move both sides of the body simultaneously, to jump on both feet or to steady a paper while writing.

Body awareness is the mental picture of one's own body parts, where they are, how they interrelate and how they move. Directionality is awareness of up, down, forward, backward, sideways, and diagonal movement and the ability to move in these directions on command.

Laterality is awareness of two sides of the body and the ability to move either side independently of the other. Examples are handwriting, cutting, and typing.

Midline crossing is the ability to use a hand, foot, or eye across the center of the body. Crossing the midline is especially important for integrating two sides of the body as well as two sides of the world.

Motor planning is the ability to organize and sequence the steps of an unfamiliar and complex body movement in a coordinated manner.

Spatial awareness is the understanding of space and "where one is" relative to the surrounding world. Children become aware of spatial relationships by moving through space. A child who crawls across the room learns more about spatial dimensions than one who is carried.

Visual Skills

Acuity, binocularity, and visual tracking are several important components of vision. A task such as writing, climbing stairs, or catching a ball requires your child to integrate many complicated visual skills and abilities.

Our book, *Growing an In-Sync Child: Simple, Fun Activities to Help Every Child Develop, Learn, and Grow*, goes into much greater depth about these crucial developmental skills. The book and its sequel, *In-Sync Activity Cards*, provide a feast of activities to get your children up and moving!

HOW TO USE OUR CALENDAR

You will often see BLANK in the instructions. This is an opportunity for you or your child to substitute your own noun, verb or adjective.

NOUN	VERB	ADJECTIVE
Door	Jump	Round
Wall	Creep	Soft
Switchplate	Roll	Rough
Tree	Slide	Violet
Rock	Leap	Striped
Puddle	Gallop	Square
Foot	Wiggle	Tiny
Elbow	Slither	Heavy
Nose	March	Shiny

A shorthand instruction, such as "Now the other knee," means go through the **entire sequence** with the other side of the body.

Modify any part of a Mini-Move to match your child's ability and comfort.

HAVE FUN!!!
— Joye and Carol

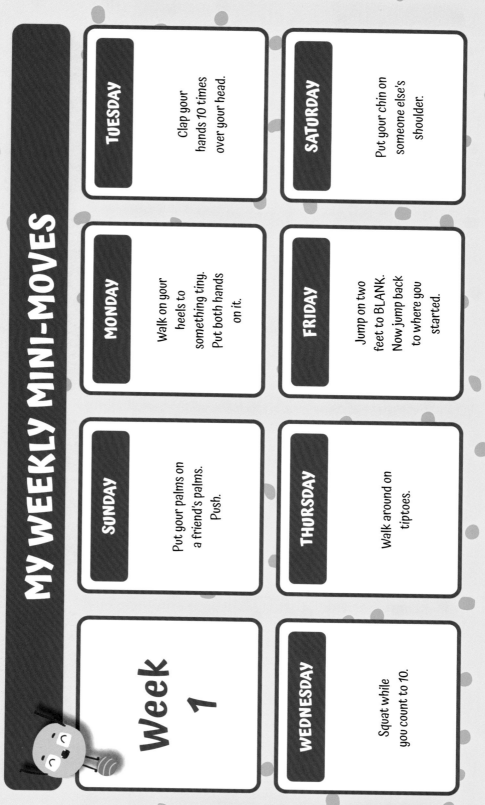

MY WEEKLY MINI-MOVES

Week 1

SUNDAY

Put your palms on a friend's palms. Push.

MONDAY

Walk on your heels to something tiny. Put both hands on it.

TUESDAY

Clap your hands 10 times over your head.

WEDNESDAY

Squat while you count to 10.

THURSDAY

Walk around on tiptoes.

FRIDAY

Jump on two feet to BLANK. Now jump back to where you started.

SATURDAY

Put your chin on someone else's shoulder.

MY WEEKLY MINI-MOVES

week 2

WEDNESDAY
Jump to something red. Put your chin on it.

SUNDAY
March in place. Clap your hands under your knee:
- left - right
- left - right

THURSDAY
Swing your arm in a BIG circle. Swing it the other way. Now the other arm.

MONDAY
Turn in a circle. Freeze. Turn the other way.

FRIDAY
Put your elbow on someone else's knee. Now put your other elbow on the person's other knee.

TUESDAY
Look over your shoulder as far behind you as you can. Turn just your head without turning your body. Count to five. Then look over your other shoulder.

SATURDAY
Try to make your body into the letter A.

A

MY WEEKLY MINI-MOVES

Week 3

SUNDAY
Carry something really heavy for 15 steps. Now go the other way.

MONDAY
Jump on both feet 10 times as loudly as you can.

TUESDAY
Pass something around your waist 10 times. Now make it go the other way.

WEDNESDAY
Slither all around on your tummy like a snake.

THURSDAY
Push against a wall or tree with both hands, as hard as you can.

FRIDAY
Raise your right knee up to your left elbow. Bring left knee to right elbow. Repeat 5 times.

SATURDAY
Stretch up to the sky. Even higher. Now flop over like a rag doll. Do it again.

MY WEEKLY MINI-MOVES

Week 4

SUNDAY
Hop on 1 foot to something square and put your nose on it.

MONDAY
Scrunch into a little baseball. Then stretch up tall into a baseball bat.

TUESDAY
Do 10 jumping jacks.

WEDNESDAY
Walk your fingers up your body from your toes to your nose. Then walk your fingers down again. Repeat a few more times.

THURSDAY
Sit on the ground and clap the soles of your feet together.

FRIDAY
Walk on an imaginary tightrope, touching the heel of one foot to the toes of the other foot.

SATURDAY
Sit on the ground facing another person, feet to feet. Hold hands. Rock forward and backward like you are on a swing.

MY WEEKLY MINI-MOVES

Week 5

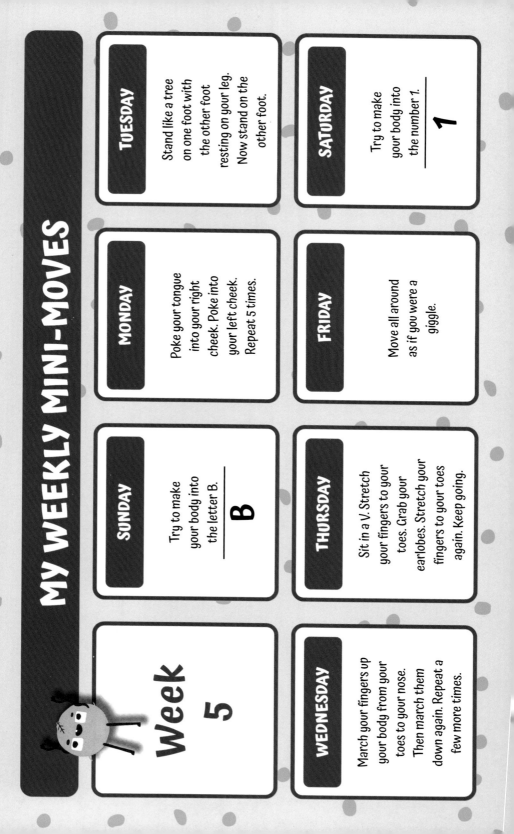

SUNDAY
Try to make your body into the letter B.

B

MONDAY
Poke your tongue into your right cheek. Poke into your left cheek. Repeat 5 times.

TUESDAY
Stand like a tree on one foot with the other foot resting on your leg. Now stand on the other foot.

WEDNESDAY
March your fingers up your body from your toes to your nose. Then march them down again. Repeat a few more times.

THURSDAY
Sit in a V. Stretch your fingers to your toes. Grab your earlobes. Stretch your fingers to your toes again. Keep going.

FRIDAY
Move all around as if you were a giggle.

SATURDAY
Try to make your body into the number 1.

1

MY WEEKLY MINI-MOVES

Week 6

SUNDAY

Sit and touch your toes to your nose. Now touch your nose to your knees.

MONDAY

Press a shoulder against a wall or a tree. Press the other shoulder. Now press your feet, one at a time. Then your hands, one at a time.

TUESDAY

Walk all around and say, "Momma Poppa Bing Bong." Tiptoe and whisper, *"Momma Poppa Bing Bong."* Stomp and shout, "MOMMA POPPA BING BONG!"

WEDNESDAY

Slide your tongue from side to side across your top teeth. Then across your bottom teeth.

THURSDAY

Creep on your hands and knees while balancing something on your back.

FRIDAY

Jump to something BLANK. Put both elbows on it.

SATURDAY

March around, touching your right hand to your left knee and your left hand to your right knee.

MY WEEKLY MINI-MOVES

Week 7

SUNDAY
Try to make your body into the letter C.

C

MONDAY
Walk backwards while counting to 5. Now walk backwards in another direction.

TUESDAY
Lying on your back, squinch your body into a tiny ball. Then explode and reach your hands and feet as far away from each other as you can.

WEDNESDAY
Make a heart shape with your hands. Now with your BLANK. Now with your whole body.

THURSDAY
Move on one foot and two hands around the space. Now go the other way.

FRIDAY
Puff air into your cheeks. Pop one cheek with one finger, then the other cheek with the other finger. Now pop both cheeks at the same time.

SATURDAY
Lie on your tummy and push up on your hands like a cobra. Look at the sky.

MY WEEKLY MINI-MOVES

Week 8

SUNDAY
BLANK to something BLANK. Put your elbow on it.

MONDAY
Lie on your back and open and close your arms. Now open and close your legs. Can you move them all together?

TUESDAY
Put your hands on the ground while a friend holds your legs. Move around like a wheelbarrow.

WEDNESDAY
Sit on the ground. Clasp your hands under your knees and rock, side to side and then forward and backward.

THURSDAY
Roll like a log.

FRIDAY
Stretch your arms out to your sides. Make 10 big arm circles. Now move your arms in the other direction 10 times.

SATURDAY
Try to make your body into the letter D.

D

MY WEEKLY MINI-MOVES

Week 9

SUNDAY
Sit on the ground and put the soles of your feet together. Touch your forehead to your toes.

MONDAY
Make your face and whole body look sad. Move sadly. Then move as if you are angry, surprised, and happy, using your whole body.

TUESDAY
Lie on your tummy and lift your arms and legs as high as you can. Hold them while you spell your name.

WEDNESDAY
Stand like a letter T. Now touch your hands overhead. Be a T again. Touch hands, be a T—10 times.

THURSDAY
Be a frog and leap from one imaginary lily pad to another.

FRIDAY
Pretend your feet are glued to the ground. Press them even harder to make sure they stick.

SATURDAY
Stand with one knee raised and pass something from one hand to the other under your knee, 6 times. Now the other knee.

MY WEEKLY MINI-MOVES

Week 10

SUNDAY
Squeeze your entire face as hard as you can while you swing your arms back and forth 10 times.

MONDAY
Hop to something green. Put both knees on it.

TUESDAY
Look straight ahead. Don't move your head as you make your eyes go all the way to the right and then all the way to the left.

WEDNESDAY
Stand. Raise one foot behind you and grab your ankle. Count to 5. Switch feet.

THURSDAY
Raise your arms to the sky and draw 10 circles. Now draw 10 circles the other way.

FRIDAY
Sit quietly on the ground with your legs in an X. Rest your hands on your knees. Listen to yourself breathe. In, out, in, out.

SATURDAY
Move sideways to something round. Put your BLANK on it.

MY WEEKLY MINI-MOVES

Week 11

SUNDAY
Try to make your body into the number 2.

2

MONDAY
Lie on your back. Clap the soles of your feet together.

TUESDAY
Grab your elbows. Swing them side to side. Can you swing them side to side over your head?

WEDNESDAY
Sit on the ground and put your hands on your head. Lean to one side as far as you can go without falling over. Now lean the other way.

THURSDAY
Try to make your body into the letter E.

E

FRIDAY
Move backwards on your hands and knees.

SATURDAY
Bend sideways and slide your hand down your leg as far as you can. Now on the other side. Keep going.

MY WEEKLY MINI-MOVES

Week 12

SUNDAY
Hold hands with a friend and jump in a circle. Now go the other way.

MONDAY
Lie on your back. Watch your thumb as you move it all around, without moving your head. Switch thumbs.

TUESDAY
Touch your ear to your shoulder. Touch your other ear to your other shoulder. Do this a few times.

WEDNESDAY
Jump 10 times as softly as you can.

THURSDAY
Sit on your bottom. Now spin in one direction. Go the other way, when you are ready.

FRIDAY
Slide to something BLANK. Put your BLANK on it.

SATURDAY
Try to make your body into the letter F.

F

MY WEEKLY MINI-MOVES

Week 13

SUNDAY
Lie on your back. Raise one foot to the sky. Switch feet. Repeat 10 times.

MONDAY
Wiggle all around the space. Now wiggle backward.

TUESDAY
Lie on your tummy. Reach back and grab your ankles. Hold on while you count backward from 12.

WEDNESDAY
Open your mouth as wide as you can. Now pucker your lips and kiss your hand. Open your mouth as wide as you can again. Now kiss your other hand.

THURSDAY
Pretend your hands are glued to your knees. Walk all around forward and backward.

FRIDAY
Raise your eyebrows. Furrow your brow. Repeat 11 times.

SATURDAY
Lie on your back and put your feet in the air. Point and flex one foot and then the other. Repeat 8 times.

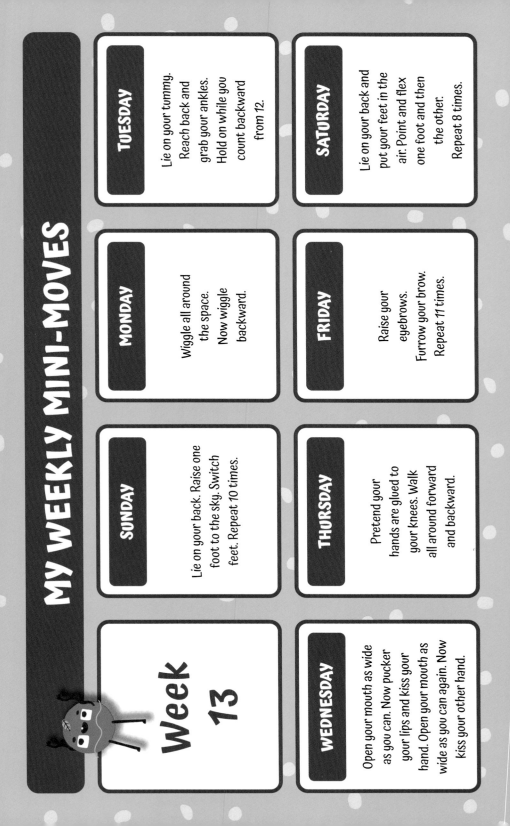

MY WEEKLY MINI-MOVES

Week 14

SUNDAY
With a friend, say "A" very quietly and then louder and louder, and then softer and softer. Say "E," "I," "O," and "U" quietly, loudly, and quietly.

MONDAY
Bounce your bottom on 3 different things. Put both hands on it.

TUESDAY
Cross your hands and pull your ears. Now stuff your earlobes into your ears.

WEDNESDAY
Touch your thumbs over your head without looking. Now touch your index fingers. Now pinkies.

THURSDAY
Try to make your body into the letter G.

G

FRIDAY
Spin on your tummy in one direction 5 times. Now spin the other way.

SATURDAY
Hold hands with yourself and swing your arms slowly side to side. Now swing quickly.

MY WEEKLY MINI-MOVES

Week 15

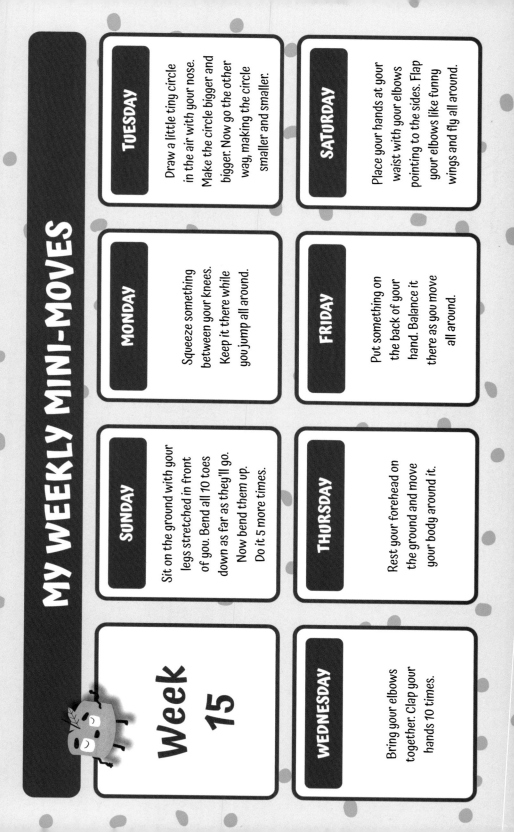

SUNDAY
Sit on the ground with your legs stretched in front of you. Bend all 10 toes down as far as they'll go. Now bend them up. Do it 5 more times.

MONDAY
Squeeze something between your knees. Keep it there while you jump all around.

TUESDAY
Draw a little tiny circle in the air with your nose. Make the circle bigger and bigger. Now go the other way, making the circle smaller and smaller.

WEDNESDAY
Bring your elbows together. Clap your hands 10 times.

THURSDAY
Rest your forehead on the ground and move your body around it.

FRIDAY
Put something on the back of your hand. Balance it there as you move all around.

SATURDAY
Place your hands at your waist with your elbows pointing to the sides. Flap your elbows like funny wings and fly all around.

MY WEEKLY MINI-MOVES

Week 16

SUNDAY

Stretch one arm overhead. Lean way over to the other side. Switch arms and lean the other way.

MONDAY

Close your eyes gently. Open them. Now scrunch them closed as tightly as you can. Repeat 5 times.

TUESDAY

Try to make your body into the number 3.

3

WEDNESDAY

Grab your wrists and pull them apart 5 times. Now switch hands and pull 5 more times.

THURSDAY

Try to make your body into the letter H.

H

FRIDAY

Tiptoe to something pink. Put one hand and one foot on it.

SATURDAY

Shrug one shoulder as high as you can without moving the other shoulder. Now shrug the other H shoulder. Repeat 10 times.

MY WEEKLY MINI-MOVES

Week 17

SUNDAY
Lie on your back and raise your bottom as high as it can go, like a bridge. Count to 5. Lower your bottom and do it again, 4 more times.

MONDAY
Slap your thighs with your hands to make a loud sound. Do it 8 times. Put both hands on your thighs.

TUESDAY
Stand on one foot with your eyes closed. Count to 5. Now on the other foot. Repeat 6 times.

WEDNESDAY
Do 5 standing-up push-ups against a tree or wall.

THURSDAY
Clap your hands 5 times. Now clap your elbows 5 times. Now clap your knees 5 times.

FRIDAY
Waddle all around like a duck. Quack if you want to.

SATURDAY
Raise both arms and swish them from side to side like windshield wipers. Wipe the whole make-believe windshield.

MY WEEKLY MINI-MOVES

week 18

SUNDAY
Move around on two feet and one hand.

MONDAY
Do 3 somersaults.

TUESDAY
Hold something under your chin and shuffle your feet all around.

WEDNESDAY
Lie on your side, as straight as a pencil. Balance as long as you can. Do it on the other side.

THURSDAY
Jump forward as far as you can on both feet together. Jump 2 more times. Now jump backward to where you started.

FRIDAY
Prance like a pony.

SATURDAY
Sit on your bottom and put your hands and feet on the ground. Raise your bottom off the ground and move all around.

MY WEEKLY MINI-MOVES

Week 19

SUNDAY
Stand with your feet together. Step one foot to the side. Bring your other foot next to it. Keep going 7 more times. Now the other way 8 times.

MONDAY
Sit on the ground and slide your heels toward your bottom. Now straighten your legs. Repeat 4 more times.

TUESDAY
Clap your hands behind your back 10 times.

WEDNESDAY
Lie on your back with your feet in the air. Pretend to pedal a bicycle.

THURSDAY
Clap one hand and one foot together 6 times. Now clap the other hand and foot.

FRIDAY
Both arms out! Bend one and touch thumb to nose. Arms out! Bend the other and touch thumb to nose. Arms out! Touch nose with both thumbs. Repeat with pointers, then pinkies.

SATURDAY
Shrug your shoulders as high as you can. Now blow out a big breath and let your shoulders relax. Repeat a few more times.

MY WEEKLY MINI-MOVES

Week 20

SUNDAY
Make a giant "X" with your body. Now squeeze yourself into a tight little ball. Count to 3 and then explode into an "X" again.

MONDAY
Be a tiny seed. Slowly grow until you're a wide-open flower, facing the sun.

TUESDAY
Slide on your feet all around. Slide backwards and sideways, too.

WEDNESDAY
Try to make your body into the letter J.

J

THURSDAY
Walk on your knees without using your hands. Try moving sideways and backward, too.

FRIDAY
Roll to something black. Put your BLANK on it.

SATURDAY
Stick out your tongue as far as it will go. Now stick it out and up. Now stick it out and down. Now to one side and then the other.

MY WEEKLY MINI-MOVES

Week 21

SUNDAY
Put your chin on your knee. Put your nose on your knee. Put your forehead on your knee. Now the other knee.

MONDAY
Try to make your body into the letter K.

K

TUESDAY
Bounce on your tiptoes 20 times.

WEDNESDAY
Stretch your arms out. Keep your feet together. Twist as far as you can to one side and then to the other side. Repeat 7 times.

THURSDAY
Stretch any way you want. Now find a different way to stretch.

FRIDAY
Be rain and then open yourself up like an umbrella.

SATURDAY
BLANK to a straight line. Put one elbow and one knee on it. Find another straight line and do it again.

MY WEEKLY MINI-MOVES

week 22

SUNDAY
Clasp your hands behind you. Lift your chin. Stretch.

MONDAY
Give yourself a few big bear hugs. Hug your shoulders. Hug your waist. Hug your knees.

TUESDAY
Beat your chest and shout the days of the week.

WEDNESDAY
Stand on one leg and swing the other leg forward and back. Do it on the other leg.

THURSDAY
Pat your thighs with your hands, one hand at a time, as if your hands are walking. Count to 17.

FRIDAY
Try to make your body into the number 4.

4

SATURDAY
Sit, legs crisscrossed. Creep your fingers forward on the ground, far away. Now creep your fingers behind you.

MY WEEKLY MINI-MOVES

Week 23

SUNDAY
With both hands, tap your thighs, tap your chin, tap your thighs, tap your nose, tap your thighs, tap your forehead. Now reverse.

MONDAY
Jump on both feet, turning in a circle. Now jump and go the other way.

TUESDAY
Squeeze your knees together while you walk around.

WEDNESDAY
Hold your hands out to the sides, palms down. Hit the air 5 times. Now palms up. Repeat sequence to front and back.

THURSDAY
Put one hand on your head and the other hand on your knee. Switch hands 10 times.

FRIDAY
Crouch and put your hands on the ground. Keep crouching and put your hands on your knees. Ground, knees, ground, knees, 5 times.

SATURDAY
Make your shoulders dance by moving one forward while you move the other one backward and then switch.

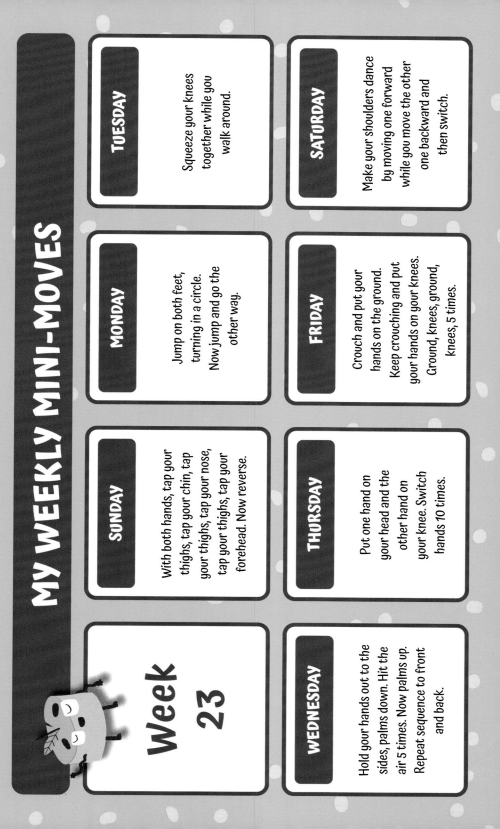

MY WEEKLY MINI-MOVES

Week 24

SUNDAY
Make noise
without using
your voice.

MONDAY
Try to make your
body into the
letter L.

TUESDAY
Squeeze your elbows
together and march
around.

WEDNESDAY
Lie on your back, put
your legs in the air,
grab your ankles, and
rock from side to side.

THURSDAY
Move on one knee
and two hands.

FRIDAY
Go outside and
count the sounds.

SATURDAY
Gallop to BLANK.
Put your BLANK
on it.

MY WEEKLY MINI-MOVES

Week 25

SUNDAY
Scoot backward.

MONDAY
Try to make your body into the letter M.

M

TUESDAY
Move like a spider.

WEDNESDAY
Put one thumb on your chin and the other thumb on your belly button. Switch. Now do it with your eyes closed and hum a song.

THURSDAY
Point one foot to the side. Tap your toes on the ground 3 times. Now point and tap the other toes to the other side.

FRIDAY
Sit down on an imaginary chair. Go as low as you can go without falling over. Stand up and sit 4 more times.

SATURDAY
Clasp your hands overhead, like a big sun. Twist as far to one side as you can, then twist to the other side.

MY WEEKLY MINI-MOVES

Week 26

SUNDAY
Say "Ahh" with your mouth open as widely as it can go. Say it quietly. Say it loudly.

MONDAY
Bend over, grab your ankles, and rock from side to side.

TUESDAY
Roll all around like a ball. Now go the other way.

WEDNESDAY
Try to make your body into the letter N.

N

THURSDAY
Get on your hands and knees. Swing one knee to your shoulder 3 times. Do it on the other side.

FRIDAY
Lie on your back and try to sit up using just one hand.

SATURDAY
Kneel. Stretch your hands behind you and touch your heels.

MY WEEKLY MINI-MOVES

Week 27

TUESDAY
Walk around very loudly and quickly. Now reverse direction.

MONDAY
Jump your fingers up your body from your toes to your nose. Then jump your fingers down again. Do it a few more times.

SUNDAY
Stretch both arms over your head. Make 10 big sweeping circles in front of your body. Now sweep them in the other direction 10 times.

SATURDAY
Find something small and put it next to something big.

FRIDAY
Move on two pointy parts of your body.

THURSDAY
Try to make your body into the number 6.

WEDNESDAY
Touch shoulder with opposite hand. Touch other shoulder with other hand. Now touch head with both hands. Repeat sequence 6 times.

MY WEEKLY MINI-MOVES

Week 28

SUNDAY
Sway your hips from side to side. Count to 12.

MONDAY
Find something BLANK and put it on top of something square.

TUESDAY
Walk around very quietly and slowly.

WEDNESDAY
Stomp to something round. Put both elbows on it.

THURSDAY
"Walk" on your bottom by shifting side to side.

FRIDAY
Kiss one shoulder. Now kiss the other shoulder. Now kiss the sky. Repeat 5 times.

SATURDAY
Stand and touch your toes with the opposite hand. Now touch your other toes with your other hand. Do it 10 times.

MY WEEKLY MINI-MOVES

Week 29

SUNDAY
Move on one elbow and two knees.

MONDAY
Try to make your body into the letter O.

O

TUESDAY
BLANK around very loudly and slowly.

WEDNESDAY
Move sideways on your hands and feet. Now go in the other direction.

THURSDAY
March in place with your eyes closed for 15 seconds.

FRIDAY
Stand on one foot and bounce up and down on your toes 10 times. Then on your other toes.

SATURDAY
Sit with your legs in front of you. Touch your toes with the opposite hand. Now touch your other toes with your other hand. Do it 10 times.

MY WEEKLY MINI-MOVES

Week 30

SUNDAY
Walk around while you spell your name. Say the letter when your foot touches the ground.

MONDAY
Stand with one foot in front of the other, toes to heel. Count to 10. Now switch feet. Count to 10 again.

TUESDAY
Lie on your tummy. Stretch your arms out in front. Pretend you are swimming, using your arms and legs.

WEDNESDAY
On your hands and knees, straighten your leg behind you and swing it to the side. Alternate legs, 8 times.

THURSDAY
Twirl around in both directions.

FRIDAY
Lie on your back. Point your toes to the sky. Criss-cross your ankles so one foot is in front and then the other foot is in front.

SATURDAY
Sit on the ground. Make a V with your legs. Touch fingers to toes.

MY WEEKLY MINI-MOVES

Week 31

SUNDAY
Lie on your tummy. Stretch one arm out to the side. Lift it and lower it 5 times. Now the other arm.

MONDAY
Try to make your body into the letter P.

P

TUESDAY
Flick a finger up and down on your lips while you say "B." Try it with different fingers.

WEDNESDAY
Stretch one hand out in front, palm up, and with the other hand press your fingers toward the ground. Switch hands. Do it twice each side.

THURSDAY
Twirl on your knees, round and round. Now twirl in the other direction.

FRIDAY
Move like an inchworm.

SATURDAY
Float all around like a balloon. When you're finished floating, pop yourself.

MY WEEKLY MINI-MOVES

Week 32

WEDNESDAY
Put your hands and knees on the ground. Keeping your arms straight, look between your legs to see what's behind you. Now look up at the sky. Repeat a few more times.

SUNDAY
Blink your eyes 10 times slowly. Now blink them 10 times fast.

THURSDAY
Try to make your body into the letter Q.

Q

MONDAY
Say the alphabet as quietly as you can. Now scream it.

FRIDAY
Lie on your back, knees bent, feet flat. Turn head one way and knees the other way. Alternate sides 6 times.

TUESDAY
Wiggle to something round. Put 3 fingers on it.

SATURDAY
Hold your elbows. Try to pull them apart.

MY WEEKLY MINI-MOVES

Week 33

SUNDAY
Stand still and close your eyes. Try not to move any parts of your body while you slowly count to 10 in your mind.

MONDAY
Draw big circles with your elbows. Now draw circles in the other direction.

TUESDAY
Crawl on your belly like an alligator.

WEDNESDAY
Make your body into a triangle.

THURSDAY
Sit on the ground, legs straight. Point the toes of one foot to the sky and then to the ground. Alternate feet, 10 times. Then both feet together, 10 times.

FRIDAY
Stand like an X. Bend forward and touch your right hand to your left foot. Now the other side. Repeat 5 times.

SATURDAY
Try to make your body into the number 5.

5

MY WEEKLY MINI-MOVES

Week 34

SUNDAY
Draw 11 giant Figure 8s in the air with your chin.

MONDAY
Look at something far away. Look at your hand. Look at something far away again. Repeat 10 times.

TUESDAY
Lie on your back. Now stand up. Now lie down again. Repeat 5 times.

WEDNESDAY
Hop 2 times on one foot, then 1 time on the other foot. Repeat 5 times. Change feet and repeat the pattern.

THURSDAY
Press your nostril closed with 1 finger. Take 3 deep breaths through the open nostril. Now the other side.

FRIDAY
Make your body into a straight line on the ground, lying on your side. Balance. Close your eyes. Switch sides.

SATURDAY
Try to make your body into the letter R.

R

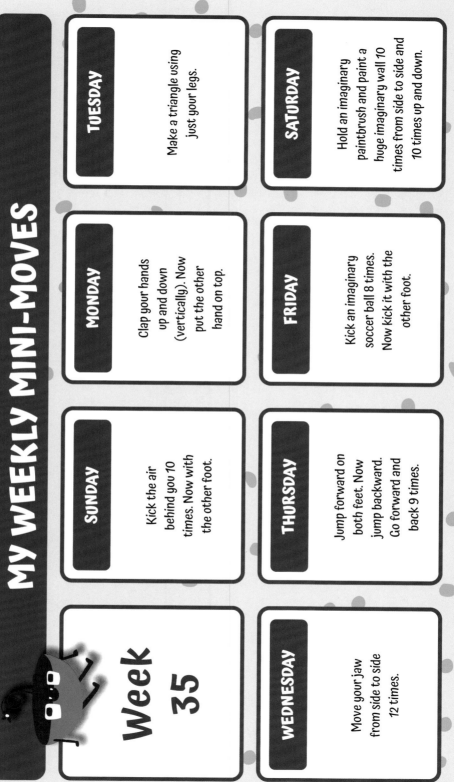

MY WEEKLY MINI-MOVES

Week 35

SUNDAY
Kick the air behind you 10 times. Now with the other foot.

MONDAY
Clap your hands up and down (vertically). Now put the other hand on top.

TUESDAY
Make a triangle using just your legs.

WEDNESDAY
Move your jaw from side to side 12 times.

THURSDAY
Jump forward on both feet. Now jump backward. Go forward and back 9 times.

FRIDAY
Kick an imaginary soccer ball 8 times. Now kick it with the other foot.

SATURDAY
Hold an imaginary paintbrush and paint a huge imaginary wall 10 times from side to side and 10 times up and down.

MY WEEKLY MINI-MOVES

Week 36

SUNDAY
Clap without letting your hands touch.

MONDAY
Flap your wings like a chicken.

TUESDAY
Throw BLANK up in the air and catch it with one hand. Now catch it with your other hand.

WEDNESDAY
Twirl to something in the shape of a BLANK. Put one foot on it.

THURSDAY
Try to make your body into the letter S.

S

FRIDAY
Throw something up in the air and catch it with your BLANK. Now catch it with your other BLANK.

SATURDAY
Hop to something BLANK. Put your bottom on it.

MY WEEKLY MINI-MOVES

Week 37

SUNDAY
Draw a giant circle using only your legs. Now go the other way. Repeat 5 times.

MONDAY
Open and close your hands 10 times. Now open and close just 1 finger, then 2, then 3, then 4 at a time.

TUESDAY
Move around in a jiggly way.

WEDNESDAY
Stomp around backward and then sideways in both directions.

THURSDAY
Move like a penguin.

FRIDAY
Starting at your wrist, squeeze one arm all the way up to your shoulder. Now start on your other wrist and do the same thing.

SATURDAY
On hands and knees, raise one hand and the opposite knee off the ground. Count to 4. Switch hand and knee. Alternate 7 times.

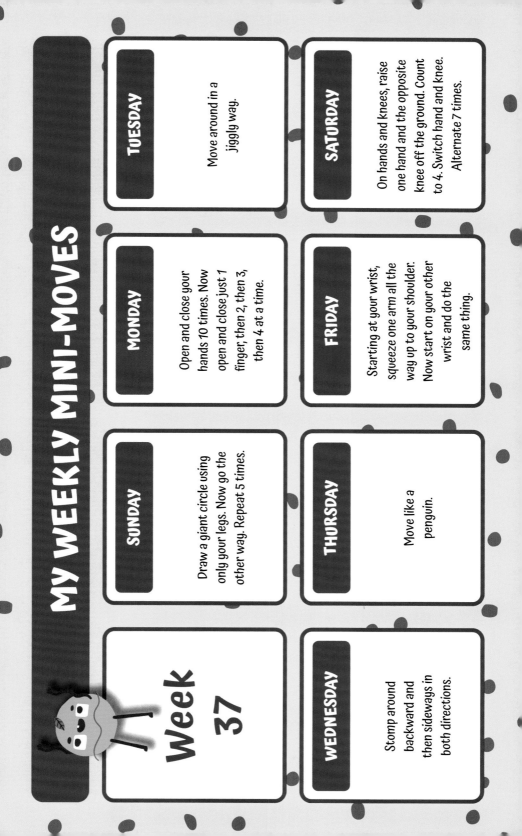

MY WEEKLY MINI-MOVES

Week 38

SUNDAY

Try to make your body into the letter T.

T

MONDAY

Shuffle sideways. Now shuffle in the other direction. Go back and forth BLANK times.

TUESDAY

Move around on only two different body parts.

WEDNESDAY

Move around stomping with one foot and being very quiet with the other foot. Switch feet and do it again.

THURSDAY

Make two big circles using one leg and one arm at the same time. Now switch.

FRIDAY

Move your eyes around in circles 3 times. Now move them the other way.

SATURDAY

Hold your thumb straight out in front of you. Now s-l-o-w-l-y bring it to your nose, watching it the whole time. Watch it as you move it back out. Now do it again with the other thumb.

MY WEEKLY MINI-MOVES

Week 39

SUNDAY
Lie on your back. Slowly roll onto your stomach. Slowly roll to your back. Roll onto stomach in the other direction. Roll to back. Twice more in each direction.

MONDAY
Watch an imaginary bubble come down from the sky. Now catch it with both hands. Catch a few more.

TUESDAY
Carry something really heavy for 15 steps. Now go the other way.

WEDNESDAY
Breathe in slowly through your nose. Blow out slowly through your mouth. Repeat 8 times.

THURSDAY
Flutter your eyelashes to give yourself a "butterfly kiss" on the back of your hand. Now "kiss" your other hand.

FRIDAY
Lift one hand over your head and touch your opposite ear. Now lift your other hand and touch your other ear. Do it a few more times.

SATURDAY
Try to make your body into the number 7.

7

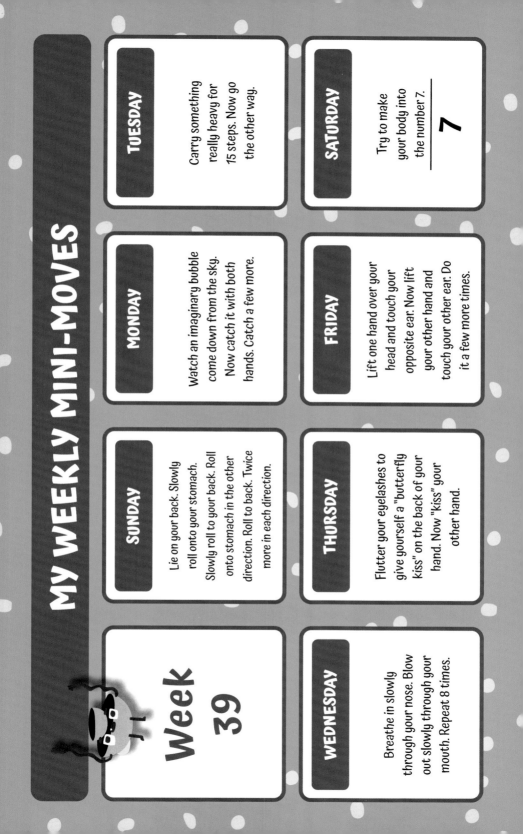

MY WEEKLY MINI-MOVES

Week 40

SUNDAY
Pat one hip with the opposite hand 5 times. Now pat your other hip with your other hand 5 times. Now put both hands behind you and pat your bottom 10 times.

MONDAY
Open one hand. Squeeze it all over with the fingers of your other hand. Now switch hands.

TUESDAY
Tilt your head as far back as you can to look at the sky. Count to 6. Now tilt your head forward to look at your toes. Count to 6. Do it again.

WEDNESDAY
Sit and drum your hands on your thighs, 1-2, 1-2, 1-2. Make a big noise!

THURSDAY
Slide on your tummy to a rectangle. Put your head on it.

FRIDAY
Bring your hands near your ears and rub your fingertips together so you can hear them.

SATURDAY
Put your back on a wall. Slide down to the ground. Get back up without using your hands.

MY WEEKLY MINI-MOVES

Week 41

SUNDAY
Scoot on your bottom. Can you scoot without using your hands?

MONDAY
Beat your chest and count backwards from 40 to 30.

TUESDAY
Smear imaginary mud all over your body.

WEDNESDAY
Try to make your body into the letter U.

U

THURSDAY
Move your arms as if they were scissors. Now move your legs that way.

FRIDAY
Clap your name by saying a letter with each clap.

SATURDAY
Move on 3 different parts of your body.

MY WEEKLY MINI-MOVES

week 42

SUNDAY
Jump your fingers up your body from your toes to your nose. Then jump them down again.

MONDAY
Stand with your toes pointed out. Raise up on your toes 10 times. Now point your toes in and raise up 10 times.

TUESDAY
Touch your head, shoulders, knees and toes with both hands at the same time. Now touch your toes, knees, shoulders and head.

WEDNESDAY
Sit on the ground, grab your knees. Rock back and forth without falling over.

THURSDAY
Stand on one leg while counting to 5. Then stand on the other leg. Now do it with your eyes closed.

FRIDAY
Roll like a log in one direction. Now roll the other way.

SATURDAY
Twist like a tree in a hurricane.

MY WEEKLY MINI-MOVES

Week 43

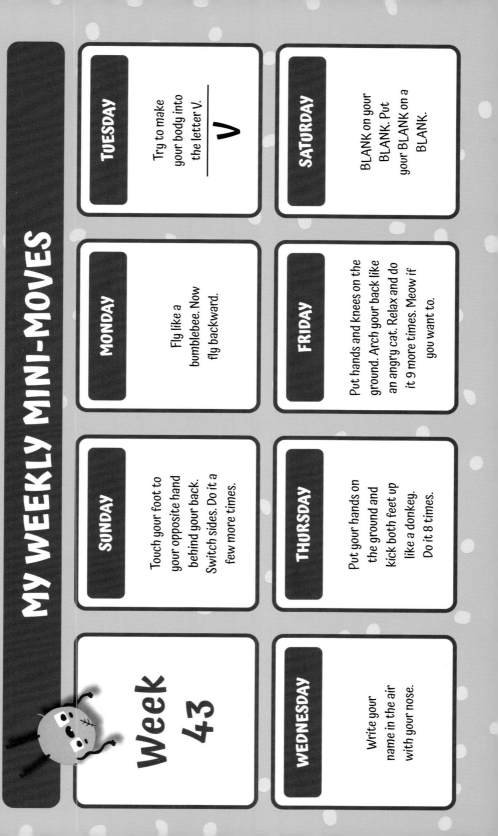

SUNDAY

Touch your foot to your opposite hand behind your back. Switch sides. Do it a few more times.

MONDAY

Fly like a bumblebee. Now fly backward.

TUESDAY

Try to make your body into the letter V.

V

WEDNESDAY

Write your name in the air with your nose.

THURSDAY

Put your hands on the ground and kick both feet up like a donkey. Do it 8 times.

FRIDAY

Put hands and knees on the ground. Arch your back like an angry cat. Relax and do it 9 more times. Meow if you want to.

SATURDAY

BLANK on your BLANK. Put your BLANK on a BLANK.

MY WEEKLY MINI-MOVES

week 44

SUNDAY
Make your body into a shape and ask a friend to copy it. Now copy your friend's shape.

MONDAY
Cross your thumbs. Wiggle your fingers like a butterfly.

TUESDAY
Slide on your back to a straight line. Put your back on it.

WEDNESDAY
Scrunch your face as hard as you can. Hold it tight. Then scream, "Boo!"

THURSDAY
Hop 10 times, counting from 1 to 10. Switch feet, counting from 10 to 1.

FRIDAY
On hands and knees, creep sideways in each direction.

SATURDAY
Spin yourself round and round on one foot. Now go the other direction. Now spin in each direction on your other foot.

MY WEEKLY MINI-MOVES

Week 45

SUNDAY
Make a circle with your thumb and pointer. Poke the other thumb into the circle. Then the other fingers, one by one. Switch hands.

MONDAY
Try to make your body into the letter W.

W

TUESDAY
Put your hands on your knees. Criss-cross your hands from knee to knee. Do it 12 times.

WEDNESDAY
Do 10 jumping jacks.

THURSDAY
BLANK to something BLANK. Put your BLANK on it.

FRIDAY
Throw something up in the air and catch it on the back of one hand. Now catch it on the back of your other hand.

SATURDAY
Climb an imaginary beanstalk.

MY WEEKLY MINI-MOVES

Week 46

SUNDAY
Lie on your back. Draw squares on the ceiling with your eyes. Go both ways.

MONDAY
Watch an imaginary bubble come down from the sky and pop it with two fingers.

TUESDAY
Try to make your body into the number 8.

8

WEDNESDAY
Lie on your back. Slide your arms on the ground, as far above your head as you can. Stretch your legs in the opposite direction. Hold the stretch while you count to 11.

THURSDAY
Bounce an imaginary ball with one hand, 5 times. Then with the other hand. Throw the ball into an imaginary basket.

FRIDAY
Be a kangaroo and jump 3 times forward and 2 times backward.

SATURDAY
Clasp your hands behind you and raise them as high as you can. Hold them there while you spell your name slowly.

MY WEEKLY MINI-MOVES

Week 47

SUNDAY

Gallop like a zebra.

MONDAY

Try to make your body into the letter X.

X

TUESDAY

Hold onto your ankles and walk all around.

WEDNESDAY

Move your eyes from side to side without moving your head. Repeat 6 times.

THURSDAY

Strut like a peacock.

FRIDAY

Whisper your name 10 times.

SATURDAY

Watch an imaginary feather float down from the sky and catch it on your knee. Do it again on your other knee.

MY WEEKLY MINI-MOVES

Week 48

WEDNESDAY
Hold a BLANK between your chin and chest without using your hands. Jump all around.

SUNDAY
Run in place while you count to 10.

THURSDAY
Kick your bottom, alternating feet, 18 times.

MONDAY
Write your name in the air with each elbow.

FRIDAY
Put your elbows on your knees and walk around.

TUESDAY
Lie on your back. Close your eyes. Count 10 deep breaths.

SATURDAY
Hug yourself really tightly.

MY WEEKLY MINI-MOVES

Week 49

SUNDAY
Sway like a tree in a breeze.

MONDAY
Try to make your body into the letter y.

y

TUESDAY
Be a snowflake.

WEDNESDAY
Beat your chest and say, "Ahhh."

THURSDAY
Skate all around.

FRIDAY
Pretend your foot is a telephone. Have a conversation with someone by talking into your foot.

SATURDAY
Do a happy dance.

MY WEEKLY MINI-MOVES

Week 50

SUNDAY
Make your body into the first letter of your name.

MONDAY
Make your body into a curved line standing up. Now make a curved line on the ground.

TUESDAY
Make your body into a straight line standing up. Now make a straight line on the ground.

WEDNESDAY
Write your name in the air with each foot.

THURSDAY
Try to make your body into the number 9.

9

FRIDAY
Touch your forehead to something soft.

SATURDAY
Hold an imaginary fishing rod. Raise it overhead and cast the imaginary worm into an imaginary river. Do it 5 times.

MY WEEKLY MINI-MOVES

Week 51

SUNDAY
March sideways to something huge. Put both feet on it.

MONDAY
Hold your hands together over your head. Pretend you are a candle. Slowly, slowly melt to the ground.

TUESDAY
Clap your hands, pat one knee, clap your hands, pat the other knee. Keep going.

WEDNESDAY
Put the soles of your feet together. Flap your knees like a bat.

THURSDAY
Try to make your body into the letter Z.

Z

FRIDAY
Cover one ear with your hand and listen to your voice say the alphabet. Now on the other side.

SATURDAY
Stir imaginary soup in an imaginary pot, 10 times in one direction and 10 times in the other. Then switch hands and stir some more.

MY WEEKLY MINI-MOVES

Week 52

WEDNESDAY
Try to make your body into the number 0.

—

0

SUNDAY
Sit. Make fists. Tap one fist on the opposite thigh. Now the other side. Repeat 10 times.

THURSDAY
Chop down an imaginary tree with at least 7 whacks. Now pile up all the wood.

MONDAY
Spread open your hands and pound on the ground 10 times.

FRIDAY
Hold one ankle behind you and hop around. Now hold the other ankle and hop back to where you started.

TUESDAY
Make 3 angels in the snow, or on the beach, or on the rug.

SATURDAY
Wave goodbye with both feet. With your elbows. With your chin. With your BLANK.

ABOUT THE AUTHORS

Joye Newman

Joye Newman's goal in life is to help people, especially young children, feel comfortable in their bodies, knowing that comfort will make almost everything easier in their lives. Joye earned her master's degree in Education and Human Development from the George Washington University with a specialty in perceptual-motor development. Integrating studies in behavioral optometry, occupational therapy, and psychology into her graduate work, she developed her unique method of therapy, which has evolved into the In-Sync Child Method. Prior to establishing her private practice, Joye was a founding member and the original Education chair of WISER (Washington Independent Services for Educational Resources), a co-founder of the Jewish Primary Day School of Washington DC (now The Milton School), and the Early Childhood Special Needs Consultant for the Board of Jewish Education. Recently, Joye has been collaborating with Carol as they focus on bringing the In-Sync Child Method to parents, schools, therapists and the world. Joye lives in Maryland, knits socks, and dotes on her three magical granddaughters.

Carol Stock Kranowitz

As a preschool teacher for 25 years, Carol observed many out-of-sync children with sensory processing differences (SPD). To help them become more competent in their work and play, she learned to identify their sensory processing challenges and steer them into early intervention. In her writings and workshops, she explains SPD's effect on children's learning and behavior, and suggests fun and functional activities. Her first book in the "Sync" series, *The Out-of-Sync Child*, has been translated into 15 languages, including Spanish and Chinese, and has sold one million copies. With Joye—and with joy—she produces materials about the In-Sync Child Method, including books, webinars, activity cards, and these weekly schedules of mini-moves for the home and classroom.